I0812953

FUN with FOOD WEBS

GRASSLAND FOOD WEBS

Written by Charis Mather

KidHaven PUBLISHING

Published in 2024 by
KidHaven Publishing, an Imprint of Greenhaven Publishing, LLC
2544 Clinton St., Buffalo, NY 14224

Written by: Charis Mather
Edited by: Rebecca Phillips-Bartlett
Designed by: Dan Scase

Image Credits
All images are courtesy of Shutterstock.com, unless otherwise specified—with thanks to Getty Images, Thinkstock Photo, and iStockphoto. Cover – SAROJ GURJAR, JaySi, Martin Prochazkacz, Joram_Njuki, GoodFocused. 4–5 – JaySi, Repina Valeriya. 6–7 – Willem in Africa, Stu Porter, Iv Nikolny, Ava Peattie, GoodFocused. 8–9 – dktirol, deva pradnyana88. 10–11 – GoodFocused, Doikanoy, John Tann, Oleg Znamenskiy. 12–13 – Dominyk Lever, Milan Zygmunt, NickEvansKZN, Ava Peattie. 14–15 – Iv Nikolny, Danita Delimont. 16–17 – AndreAnita, Stu Porter. 18–19 – Wayne Marinovich, Martin Pelanek. 20–21 – Willem in Africa, Alta Oosthuizen. 22–23 –EcoPrint, nwdph, Dennis W Donohue, Willem in Africa, Stu Porter, Iv Nikolny, Ava Peattie, GoodFocused, NickEvansKZN, Martin Pelanek, Dominyk Lever.

Cataloging-in-Publication Data

Names: Mather, Charis, 1999-.
Title: Grassland food webs / Charis Mather.
Description: Buffalo, New York: KidHaven Publishing, 2024. |
Series: Fun with food webs | Includes glossary and index.
Identifiers: ISBN 9781534546028 (pbk.) | ISBN 9781534546035 (library bound) |
ISBN 9781534546042 (ebook)
Subjects: LCSH: Grassland ecology--North America--Juvenile literature. |
Food chains (Ecology)--North America--Juvenile literature.
Classification: LCC QH102.M38 2024 | DDC 577.4--dc23

Manufactured in the United States of America

CPSIA compliance information: Batch #CW24KH: For further information contact Greenhaven Publishing LLC at 1-844-317-7404.

Please visit our website, www.greenhavenpublishing.com.
For a free color catalog of all our high-quality books, call toll free 1-844-317-7404 or fax 1-844-317-7405.

Find us on

CONTENTS

Words that look like ***THIS*** can be found in the glossary on page 24.

The Grassland Ecosystem

Grasslands might seem like they are just big empty fields, but they are actually home to many living things. Grasslands are not as dry as deserts but not as wet as forests.

Grasslands have different names around the world. African grasslands are savannas.

These open areas are full of grass, plants, and animals. Together, these things make up the grassland **ECOSYSTEM**. Every living thing in the ecosystem needs other living things to survive.

Food Chains and Food Webs

All grassland animals need to eat, which makes them part of a food chain. Food chains show what eats what in an ecosystem.

a savanna food chain

If a living thing eats or is eaten by many different living things, it can be part of many food chains. When different food chains from one ecosystem are connected, a food web is formed.

PRODUCERS

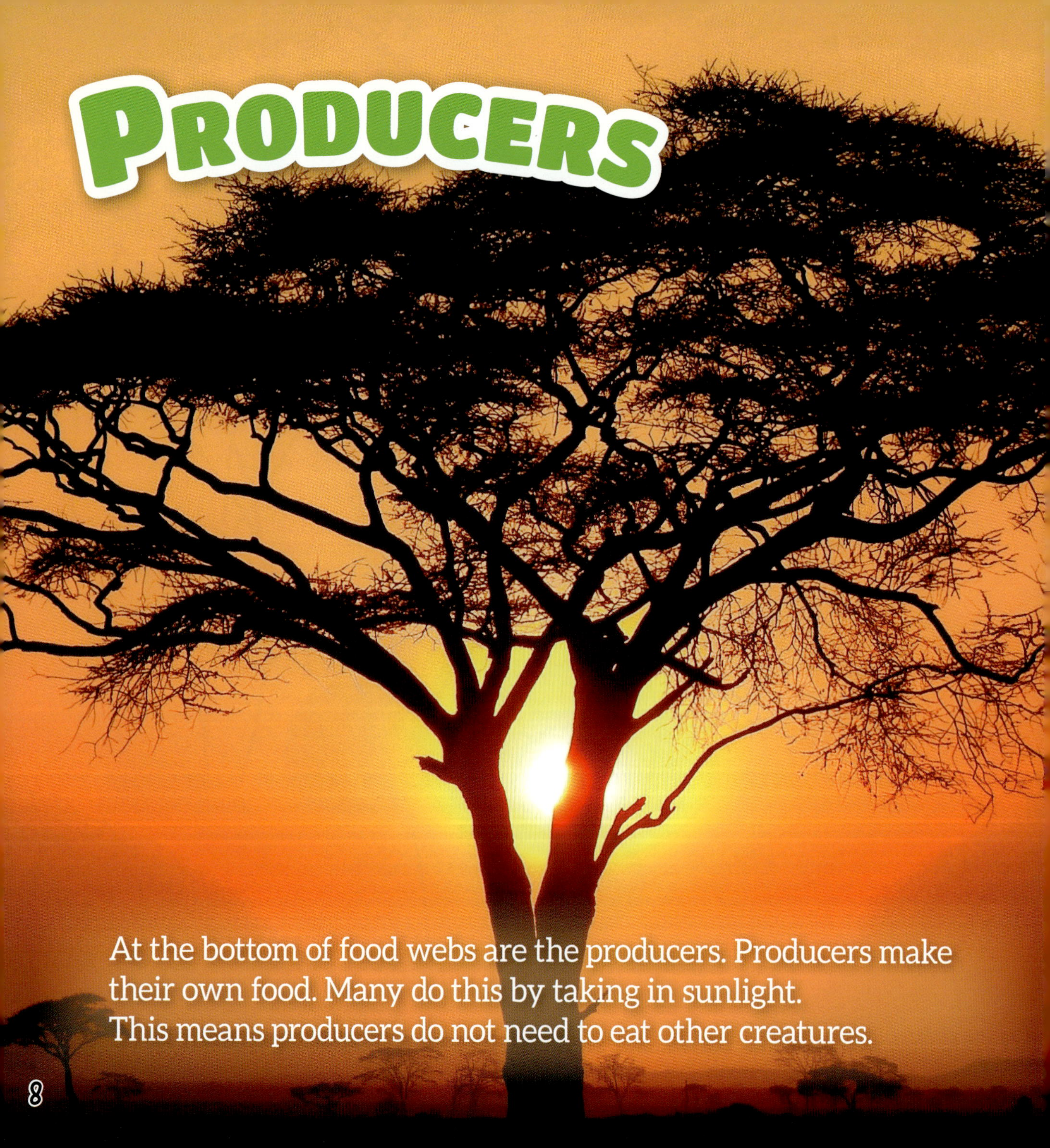

At the bottom of food webs are the producers. Producers make their own food. Many do this by taking in sunlight. This means producers do not need to eat other creatures.

Plants are one type of producer. They are an excellent **source** of food for many grassland animals. Grasses are the main producers in this ecosystem, but there are also some trees and bushes.

GRASSES

Grasslands are not just made up of one type of grass. Below are some grasses found in different grassland areas around the world.

The savanna's many types of grasses **SUPPORT** many large **GRAZING** animals. Zebras, wildebeests, and antelopes are just some of the animals that eat grass.

FOOD:	EATEN BY:
made with the help of sunlight	insects, zebras, wildebeests, antelopes, hares

Consumers

Living things that eat other living things are called consumers. If consumers only eat plants, they are herbivores. Consumers that eat meat are carnivores. If they eat both meat and plants, they are omnivores.

INSECTS

FOOD: mostly grasses, leaves, seeds (some eat meat)	**EATEN BY:** mongooses, snakes, lizards, frogs, birds

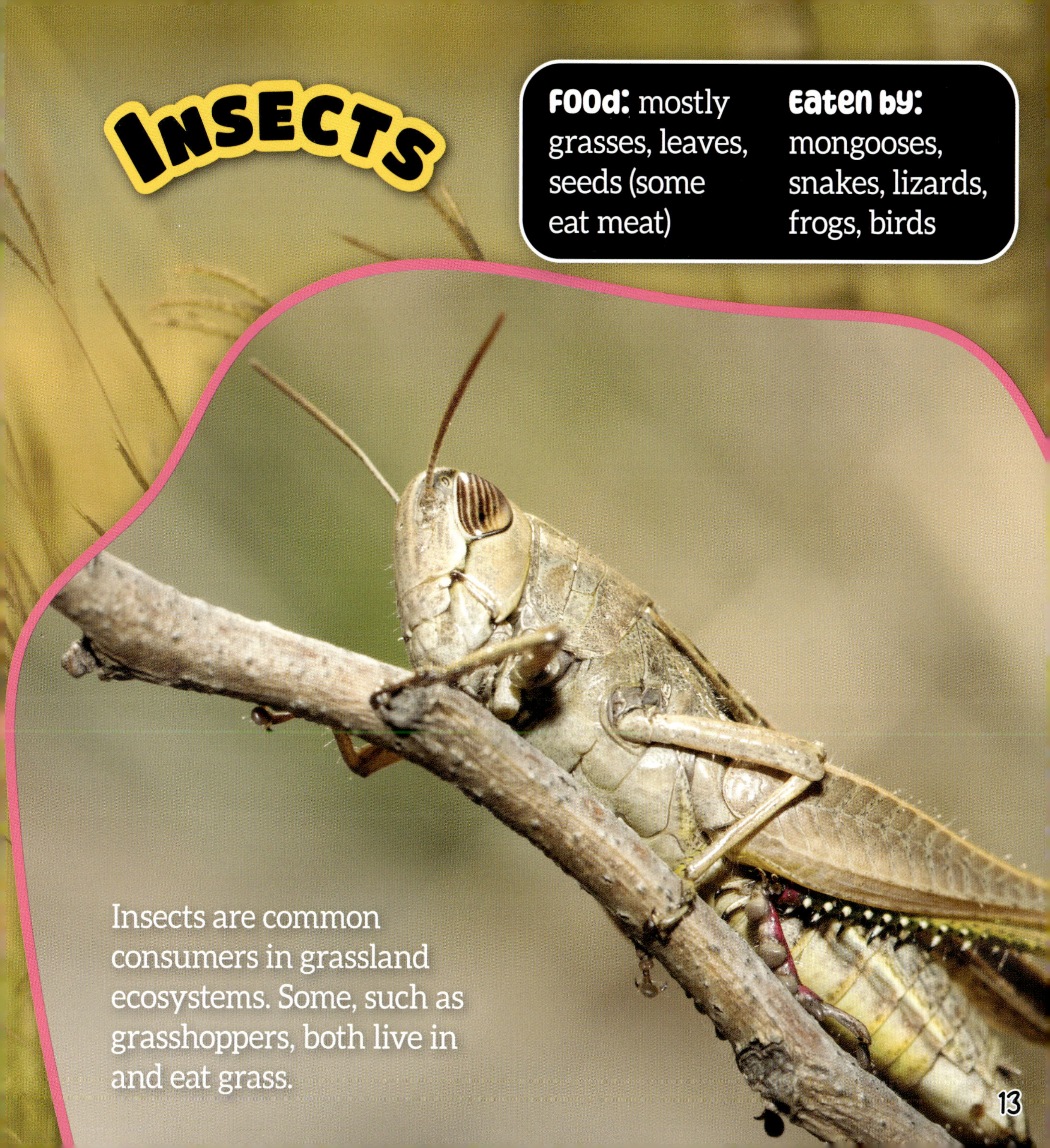

Insects are common consumers in grassland ecosystems. Some, such as grasshoppers, both live in and eat grass.

MONGOOSES

Mongooses are not fussy about food. They will go after all sorts of small animals. Some mongooses even hunt snakes. Mongooses are omnivores, so they also eat some plants.

Even though mongooses are ***PREDATORS***, they still have to look out for other predators that might eat them. To stay safe, many mongooses live in dens made from ***TERMITE*** nests.

CARACALS

Caracals are speedy hunters. They are strong jumpers and can leap about 10 feet (3 m) high to catch birds. Their golden coats help them stay hidden from their **PREY** while they hunt.

FOOD: mongooses, snakes, hares, lizards, birds

EATEN BY: lions, hyenas

If a caracal has caught a meal that is too big for it to eat all at once, it may keep the rest for later. Sometimes, caracals ***STASH*** their prey up in a tree.

Apex Predators

Apex predators are consumers that sit at the top of food webs. These hunters are not food for any other creature in their ecosystem. Instead, they hunt lots of animals lower down in the food web.

Hyenas

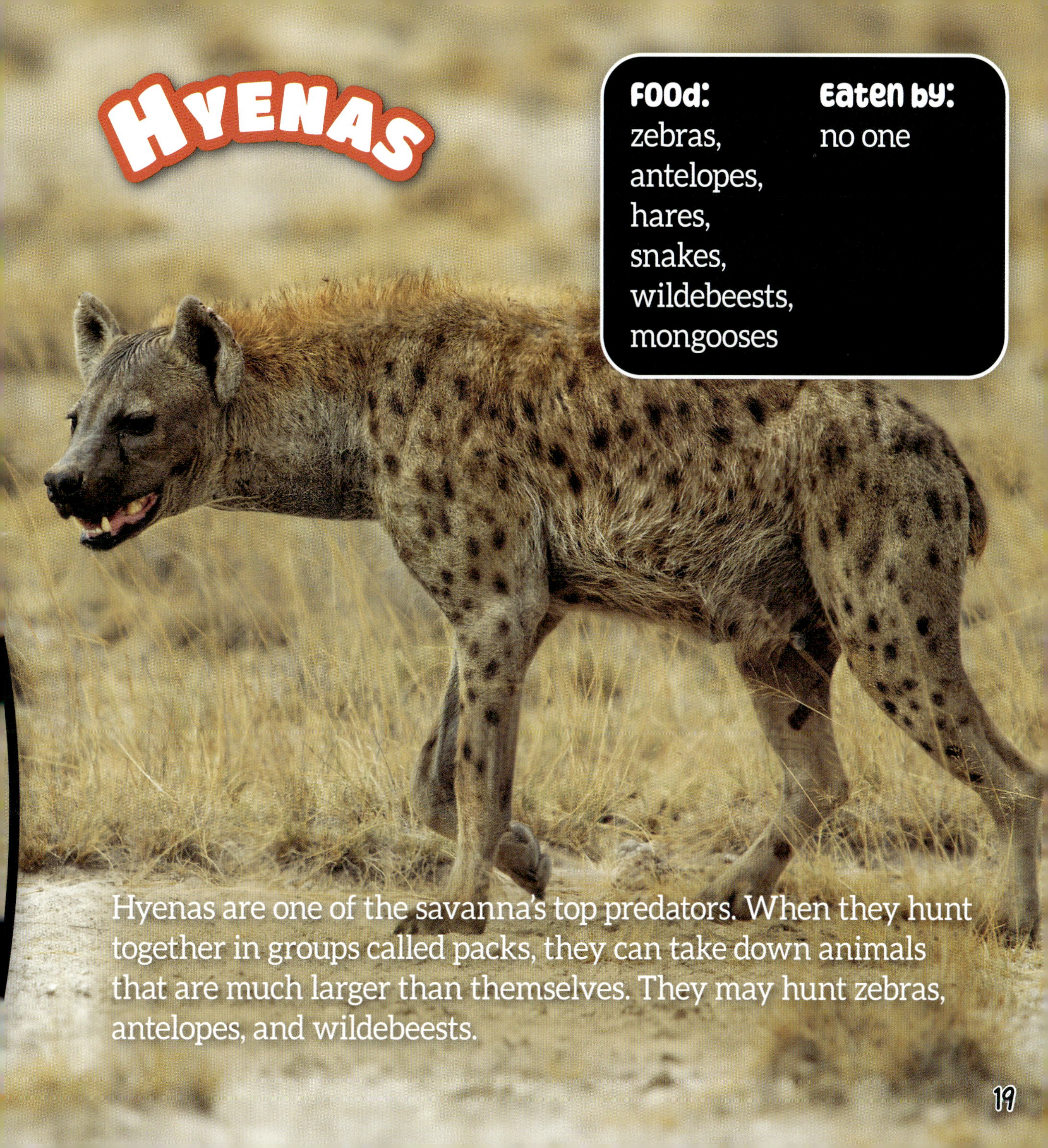

Food:	Eaten by:
zebras, antelopes, hares, snakes, wildebeests, mongooses	no one

Hyenas are one of the savanna's top predators. When they hunt together in groups called packs, they can take down animals that are much larger than themselves. They may hunt zebras, antelopes, and wildebeests.

Lions

Few animals on the savanna are as dangerous as lions. These apex predators only eat meat. They get their food from animals such as antelopes and wildebeests.

Although they are not the fastest animals in the grasslands, lions can be very ***PATIENT*** and will wait for their food. They hide in the tall grass until their prey is close enough. Then, they ***POUNCE***.

FOOD: caracals, antelopes, zebras, wildebeests

EATEN BY: no one

A GRASSLAND FOOD WEB

Look at this food web to see how ***ENERGY*** moves through the savanna. Start with the producers at the bottom, and follow the arrows. They show which living things are food for others.

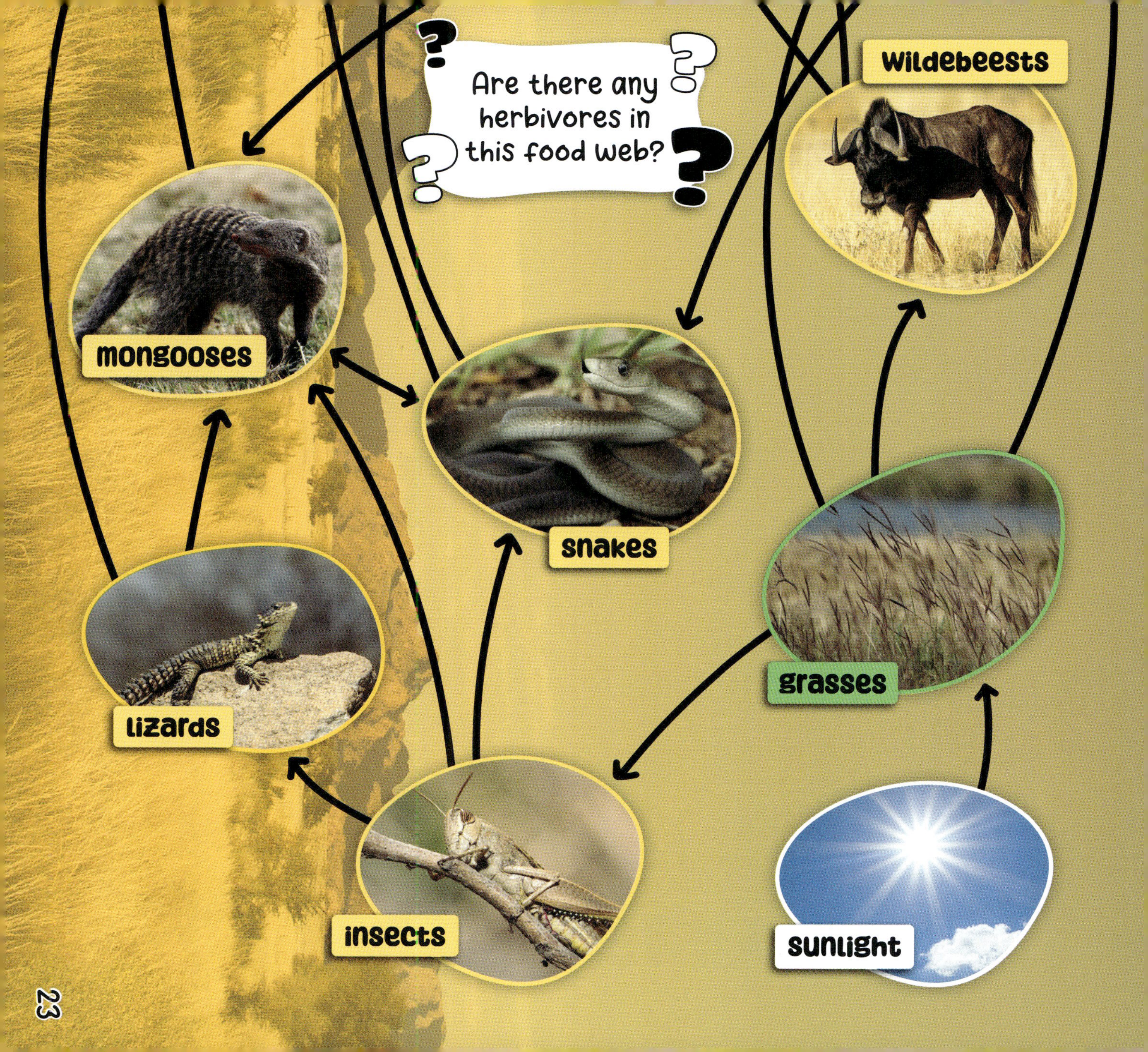

Are there any herbivores in this food web?

GLOSSARY

ecosystem a community of living things and the environment they live in

energy the power and ability to do work

grazing eating grass from a field

patient willing to wait for something

pounce to jump or spring suddenly

predators animals that hunt other animals for food

prey animals that are hunted by other animals for food

source people, places, or things from which something comes

stash to keep or store

support help

termite a small insect that eats wood and often builds large nests in the grasslands

INDEX